SPOTLIGHT ON NATIVE AMERICANS

COMANCHE

David Lee

PowerKiDS
press.

New York

Published in 2016 by The Rosen Publishing Group, Inc.
29 East 21st Street, New York, NY 10010

First Edition

Book Design: Samantha DeMartin
Reviewed by: Robert J. Conley, Former Sequoyah Distinguished Professor at Western Carolina University and Director of Native American Studies at Morningside College and Montana State University. Supplemental material reviewed by: Donald A. Grinde, Jr., Professor of Transnational/American Studies at the State University of New York at Buffalo.

Photo Credits: Cover, UniversalImagesGroup/Universal Images Group/Getty Images; p. 4 (inset) Charly Triballeau/AFP/Getty Images; pp. 4–5 (main), 10–11 DEA Picture Library/De Agostini/Getty Images; pp. 6–7 Tupungato/Shutterstock.com; p. 9 Marzolino/Shutterstock.com; p. 13 Underwood Archives/Archive Photos/Getty Images; p. 14 Buyenlarge/Archive Photos/Getty Images; p. 15 Heritage Auctions/Wikimedia Commons; p. 17 Interim Archives/Archive Photos/Getty Images; p. 18 Smithsonian American Art Museum/Wikimedia Commons; p. 19 Frederic Lewis/Archive Photos/Getty Images; p. 20 FA2010/Wikimedia Commons; p. 21 Kathryn Scott Osler/Denver Post/Getty Images; p. 22 Rick Browne/AP Images; p. 23 ullstein bild/Getty Images; p. 25 J. Scott Applewhite/AP Images; p. 26 Jason Merritt/Getty Images Entertainment/Getty Images; p. 27 MPI/Archive Photos/Getty Images; p. 29 Theo Westenberger/Hulton Archive/Getty Images.

Library of Congress Cataloging-in-Publication Data

Lee, David, 1990-
 Comanche / David Lee.
     pages cm. — (Spotlight on Native Americans)
 Includes index.
 ISBN 978-1-5081-4140-2 (pbk.)
 ISBN 978-1-5081-4141-9 (6 pack)
 ISBN 978-1-5081-4143-3 (library binding)
 1. Comanche Indians—History—Juvenile literature. 2. Comanche Indians—Social life and customs—Juvenile literature. I. Title.
 E99.C85L43 2016
 978.004'974572—dc23
                                    2015025083

Manufactured in the United States of America

CPSIA Compliance Information: Batch #BW16PK: For Further Information contact Rosen Publishing, New York, New York at 1-800-237-9932

CONTENTS

THE FIRST PEOPLES

CHAPTER 1

More than 500 Native American groups make their home in the United States, with even more living in Canada. The Comanches are a people who live in Oklahoma. But who are Native Americans, and how do Comanches fit into the history of North America's native peoples?

Ancestors of Native Americans migrated, or moved, to North America more than 12,000 years ago, probably at a time when sea levels were low enough to uncover dry land in the area between northeastern Asia and Alaska.

The first peoples in North America moved around the continent in small groups, hunting wild animals and collecting a wide variety of plant foods. They developed separate **cultures** based on their **environments**. Over time, some started to grow crops, which allowed for the development of settlements and permanent housing.

It wasn't until around AD 1500 that European ships reached North America. The newcomers brought guns and horses, which were a threat but also were useful to the Comanches. The Comanche lifestyle began to change, and they were suddenly brought into conflict with Europeans and with other native peoples.

Native Americans, such as the Comanches, faced **persecution** from the Europeans. Many were forced to live on **reservations** and give up their native language.

COMANCHE ORIGINS

CHAPTER 2

The origin of the Comanches is an important story that's been passed down for hundreds of years. It tells of a time when great swirling winds from the four directions kicked up dust in a giant storm. The wind created people with the power of storms and the strength of the earth from which they'd been made.

Some think the Comanche name is of Spanish origin—*camino ancho*. This means "the broad trail," which refers to the trails the Comanches used for **raids**. Others think it comes from an Ute word that means "enemy." The Comanches call themselves Nerm (sometimes Numinu, Neum, or Nununuh), which means "the people" or "people of people."

In the 1600s, the Comanches migrated from what's now central Wyoming to areas in modern-day Colorado and Kansas. Finally, they moved to the southern Great Plains. In the 1700s and 1800s, the Comanches were a powerful presence in the southern Great Plains, in an area that stretched from present-day eastern New Mexico across central Oklahoma and southern Kansas to today's central Texas. They guarded their land and led bloody raids that stretched even into Mexico.

Rocky Mountains

The Comanche language is nearly the same as that of the Northern Shoshones. It belongs to the Uto-Aztecan language family.

COMANCHES ON THE MOVE

CHAPTER 3

The Comanches were originally hunters and gatherers who lived in the northern Rocky Mountains in Wyoming. They hunted elk and deer on foot. However, when the Europeans brought horses in the late 1600s, the Comanche lifestyle changed. On horseback, the Comanches became great bison hunters who were able to follow and attack large herds.

This change began the Comanche migration south, as they followed bison herds. By the early 1700s, the Spanish began encountering Comanches in what is now southeastern Colorado. The Comanche migration alarmed the Spanish because it threatened to upset Native American relations in New Mexico. The Spanish had made friends with the Plains Apaches, but they were in danger of being driven off the southern Great Plains by the arrival of the Comanches.

The Plains Apaches asked for help from the Spanish, who built a fort for them. Nothing could stop the Comanches though—they numbered in the thousands. Around 1724, bands of Plains Apaches fought in a great battle against the Comanches, but they lost. In the years following, Comanches gained complete control of the southern Great Plains.

The Comanches gained great power from owning horses. They became masters of hunting and of raiding villages and settlements on horseback.

COMANCHES AND THE SPANISH

CHAPTER 4

During the mid-1700s, the Spanish lived in settlements in the regions that are now Texas and New Mexico. They were prime targets for Comanche raids. There were so many Comanches—and so few Spanish soldiers—that Comanches raided Spanish ranches at will, stealing horses by the thousands.

In 1787, fighting ended when the Comanches became military **allies** of the Spanish in New Mexico. For the time, there was peace in the region. The Comanches helped the

Spanish fight the Apaches, the former allies of the Spanish. The Apaches began raiding Spanish cattle herds after the Comanches had taken the bison off the plains.

The peace between the Spanish and Comanches ended during the Mexican War of Independence, which lasted from 1810 to 1821. After the Spanish settlers won their independence from Spain and formed Mexico, Comanches no longer saw them as allies and returned to their raids.

In 1848, the United States defeated Mexico in a war and acquired New Mexico as a territory. In 1845, Texas also became a U.S. state. The Comanches had a new and more powerful enemy to fight.

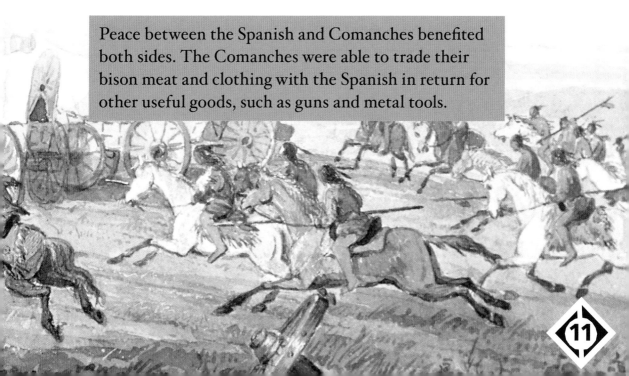

Peace between the Spanish and Comanches benefited both sides. The Comanches were able to trade their bison meat and clothing with the Spanish in return for other useful goods, such as guns and metal tools.

THE UNITED STATES TAKES OVER

CHAPTER 5

As Texas and New Mexico came under U.S. authority, new conflicts began. In the beginning, the United States mostly defended itself from attacks. The U.S. Army built a line of forts across the Texas frontier. However, that didn't stop the Comanches from traveling around the region.

After the American Civil War, the U.S. Army became more **aggressive**. Large armies defeated some Comanche bands. The Comanches were forced to move to a reservation under the Medicine Lodge **Treaty** (1867). Under the treaty, the U.S. government promised to provide Comanches with food, but the United States didn't hold up that part of the deal. Many Comanches returned to the plains.

In 1874, the U.S. Army launched a massive campaign, with many soldiers coming from forts in all directions. The soldiers had cannons and an early kind of machine gun. The Comanches were forced to flee their villages, which the soldiers then burned. That winter, when the Comanches were starving and freezing, they had no choice but to surrender. U.S. hide hunters killed the rest of the bison, forcing the Comanches to give up their way of life.

In 1858, a special group of white fighters called the Texas Rangers led surprise attacks on Comanche villages, killing many.

FORCED FROM THEIR LAND

CHAPTER 6

The Comanches, who had once ridden freely across the Great Plains, found themselves stuck in present-day southwestern Oklahoma. Their reservation was located near the dry, rocky Wichita Mountains, on land that wasn't suitable for farming. The United States forced them to become farmers anyway. Comanche children were taken to schools far away to break them of their **customs** and traditions.

Although U.S. treaties promised that Comanches

would have their reservation forever, the land was soon given to white settlers. In 1892, Congress forced the Comanches to accept individual ownership of small farms. The rest of the land was sold.

The 1900s were a hard time for the Comanches. Americans forced them to assimilate, or become more like white people, and their culture was nearly lost.

In 1907, the Comanches were forced to become citizens of the state of Oklahoma. The U.S. government argued that the Comanche Nation no longer existed. It wasn't until 1934 that the government allowed Comanches to officially join the Kiowa and Kiowa-Apache peoples to form a sort of government for themselves. In the 1960s, the Comanches were finally able to organize their own nation.

Quanah Parker was a famous Comanche war chief during the late 1800s and a **diplomat** between the Comanches and the U.S. government. Parker became an influential leader of Native Americans on national issues.

COMANCHE DIVISION AND PARTNERSHIP

CHAPTER 7

It wasn't until they were forced to live on a reservation that the Comanches formed one political identity. Over the past several hundred years, they sometimes had as few as three tribal divisions and sometimes as many as 12. Each operated as an independent unit, with different territory on the bison plains.

By the mid-1800s, they had six divisions: Kwahada (antelope), Penatekas (honey eaters), Tenewa (downstream people), Nokoni (wanderers), Kotsotekas (buffalo eaters), and Yamparika (root eaters). Each warrior society was capable of organized military efforts, unlike many other Plains peoples.

The Kiowa people were strong allies of the Comanches. Around 1790, the Comanches and Kiowas declared peace with each other. The two groups traveled, hunted, and fought together against common enemies. However, they couldn't have been more different.

The Kiowas thought the Comanches were too hotheaded, while the Comanches thought the Kiowas would rather talk about a problem than face it. Despite those differences, they remained great partners for many years.

This photograph, taken around 1891, shows a Kiowa warrior named Elk Tongue on horseback.

COMANCHE TRADITIONS

CHAPTER 8

Bison were a key part of the traditional Comanche way of life. In fact, the Comanches' traditional economy was based on hunting the great herds of bison on the southern Great Plains. The bison provided for almost all the Comanches' needs, from bowstrings to glue. Bison meat provided more than fresh food—it could also be stored for winter food or trail food. Comanches cut the meat into thin strips, salted it, and hung it in the sun to make dried meat that would last a long time.

Comanches used bison skin, or hides, to make clothing and warm winter blankets. They also used it to make tepees, or homes they could move from place to place. Bison meat and hides gave the Comanches valuable items for trade, especially with the Spanish and the Pueblo Indians of New Mexico.

The Comanches also traded horses. They had a seemingly endless supply of horses from their raids to sell to native groups farther north, all the way to Canada. From the mid-1700s to the mid-1800s, Comanches may have been the wealthiest and most powerful Native American group around.

This image shows a Comanche chief speaking to his people. In the background are tepees, which were traditional portable dwellings for the Comanches.

COMANCHE CREATIONS

CHAPTER 9

The Comanches weren't focused only on hunting and raiding, however. They also created beautiful works of art. Comanches were skilled at making parfleches, which are finely crafted containers made of tanned elk hide. Colored with natural dyes and decorated with beadwork and porcupine quills, many parfleches are masterpieces.

The Comanches also created clothing using deer and elk hides. Their shirts, dresses, and moccasins were finely crafted and beautifully decorated. Comanches took great pride in their appearance.

Many of the historic craft items in museums and private collections were stolen from families during the period when Comanches were being forced to accept reservation life. Soldiers, Native American agents, and settlers stole items. Traditional clothing was taken from Comanche children when they were forced to attend boarding schools. Many of those items ended up in museums.

The Comanches also created games. One traditional example is a dice game, made with dice carved from pieces of bone. One of their favorite games was called the hand game, which involved teams of players hiding a small object from each other.

Museums have the tools to restore and preserve important Comanche art and clothing.

21

COMANCHE BELIEFS

CHAPTER 10

The Comanches are a very spiritual people, and their beliefs affect their everyday lives. Traditional Comanches believe in an afterlife and worship the Great Spirit. They seek **visions** to help guide them in life.

Medicine men were very important figures in Comanche culture. They treated illnesses, interpreted dreams, and guided the nation in times of crisis. However, in 1874, a young Comanche medicine man, Isatai, told people that if the Comanches held a Sun Dance, they would be

safe from the bullets of the American hide hunters. The Comanches performed the dance and then attacked a group of hide hunters at Adobe Walls, Texas. Several Comanches were shot. After this, Comanche medicine men lost much of their influence with their peoples.

Many Native American peoples have stories that connect them to their past and to nature. One Comanche story tells of a character named Coyote that wanted to release bison from a creature called Humpback who kept all bisons caged. Coyote tricked Humpback into thinking he was a puppy Humpback's son could have as a pet. Coyote went into Humpback's dwelling and released the bison for all native peoples to use.

Quanah Parker

In the 1880s, Quanah Parker helped found a religious group that later became known as the Native American Church.

COMANCHE NATION OF OKLAHOMA

CHAPTER 11

The Comanche people of today live a very different life than those of the past, but they try to keep their heritage alive. For nearly a hundred years after the Medicine Lodge Treaty of 1867, the Comanches were formally joined with the Kiowa and Kiowa-Apache peoples. During much of the 1900s, they worked together in a business committee made up of representatives from each group.

However, in 1963, the Comanches organized the Comanche Nation of Oklahoma. Their headquarters is located north of the small city of Lawton, near the Wichita Mountains of southwestern Oklahoma. Today, around half of the nation's 15,000 members live in this region. The nation elects its leaders every three years and even has its own license plates.

Ever since 1901, when the government forced Comanches to have small individual farms instead of shared land, the Comanches have been scattered throughout their former reservation. They often mix in with the population of small towns in southwestern Oklahoma. Most children attend public schools. Some Comanches even moved away from the area to find a new life.

This picture shows Wallace Coffey, chairman of the Comanche Nation in Oklahoma. He's shown wearing a headdress in Washington, D.C., on November 20, 2013, before he attended a Congressional Gold Medal ceremony. Native Americans were honored at the ceremony for helping the United States through the use of their language to form codes during World War II.

FINDING SUCCESS

CHAPTER 12

Today, some Comanches use their creativity to express concerns and issues shared by many Native Americans. Comanche writer Cornel Pewewardy is one of the most active Native American writers trying to get Americans to stop using Native Americans as **mascots** for sports teams. His articles on that issue have appeared in many publications. He's currently a professor of Native American studies at Portland State University in Oregon. Pewewardy also performs traditional Comanche flute music.

Gil Birmingham

Comanche poet Juanita Pahdopony has been an inspiration to young Comanche writers. She is a renowned poet, artist, and teacher. Comanche actor Gil Birmingham acted in the *Twilight* movies as the character Billy Black.

Paul Chaat Smith coauthored one of the most influential books about the American Indian Movement (AIM) of the late 1960s and early 1970s. His book, *Like a Hurricane*, describes how AIM members staged protests in the United States that brought worldwide attention to the poverty and hopelessness on many reservations. In 2001, Smith became associate **curator** of the Smithsonian's National Museum of the American Indian in Washington, D.C.

Comanche writer LaDonna Harris published articles about how Comanches could start businesses and create jobs for their people. In 1965, she founded an organization called Oklahomans for Indian Opportunity.

KEEPING CULTURE ALIVE

CHAPTER 13

Though the Comanches faced persecution for many years, their culture is very much alive. In the last few decades, they've experienced a cultural **revival**. After over a century of intense attempts by the U.S. government to make them give up their traditional ways and blend into the larger European American culture, Comanches are now allowed to publicly embrace their traditions again. It's a huge change from their years of suffering, when most Americans assumed that both the Comanche people and their culture would disappear forever.

In 1972, one of the old Comanche warrior societies, the Little Pony Society, was revived to honor returning Comanche Vietnam War veterans. In 1976, the Yamparika division of the Comanches revived their Black Knives Society. Once made up of some of the best warriors in the nation, those societies had been inactive for nearly a century.

While many Comanches are reestablishing their cultural roots, others have become part of the wider American society. The most valuable resource of the Comanche Nation is its people. They have endured enormous hardships and have survived. Today, the Comanche Nation looks to the future with hope for their continued greatness.

These Comanche performers go through the steps of the Shield Dance, which depicts a clash over territory, at the American Indian Dance Theater in New York City.

GLOSSARY

aggressive: Acting with forceful energy and determination.

ally: One of two or more people or groups who work together.

culture: The beliefs and ways of life of a group of people.

curator: A person whose job it is to care for something. Curators often work in museums or places with other kinds of exhibits.

custom: An action or way of behaving that's usual and traditional among people in a certain group.

diplomat: A person who is skilled at talks between nations.

environment: The conditions that surround a living thing and affect the way it lives.

mascot: A person, animal, or object used as a symbol to represent a group and bring good luck.

persecution: The act of making a group of people suffer cruel or unfair treatment.

raid: A sudden attack.

reservation: Land set aside by the government for a specific Native American group or groups to live on.

revival: The growth or increase in the activity of something after a long period of no growth or activity.

treaty: An agreement among nations or peoples.

vision: Something that you see or dream, especially as part of a supernatural experience.

FOR MORE INFORMATION

BOOKS

Gibson, Karen Bush. *Native American History for Kids: With 21 Activities*. Chicago, IL: Chicago Review Press, 2010.

Lacey, T. Jensen. *The Comanche*. New York, NY: Chelsea House Publishers, 2011.

Sanford, William R. *Comanche Chief Quanah Parker*. Berkeley Heights, NJ: Enslow Publishers, 2013.

WEBSITES

Due to the changing nature of Internet links, PowerKids Press has developed an online list of websites related to the subject of this book. This site is updated regularly. Please use this link to access the list: www.powerkidslinks.com/sona/coman

INDEX